FOREWORD

In the last fifteen years much has been written about the process of education. The methodologies and ideas for improving achievement have come and gone often in a cyclical fashion, with each new generation of teachers rediscovering what really works in the classroom. More recently, with the advent of highly sophisticated neurological research techniques a vast amount of evidence now exists which assists our understanding of how the brain works and how learning really takes place. This evidence has been coupled with a shift in focus within our classrooms from the teacher teaching to the pupil learning. As the teaching profession uses this knowledge to develop learning and teaching strategies which can accelerate pupils' achievement, then a new partnership is being forged between teacher and pupil. This partnership is one where the responsibility for learning is increasingly in the domain of the pupil, supported and guided by the teacher. It is based on a sharing of the knowledge of how the brain works and how learning takes place. Once in possession of this knowledge and equipped with a range of learning strategies to suit the individual, the pupil can take more control of the learning process, set appropriate targets to improve achievement and experience the enjoyment of successful learning. This partnership is an essential prerequisite for raising self-esteem and achievement.

This book sets out to share some of the evidence of how learning occurs with fellow professionals in education and to highlight some of the strategies which have been in use in some of our schools in recent years. The material is laid out in an informal manner allowing teachers to "dip in" and "cherry pick" from its contents. There is something to suit every teaching style and learning preference, so enjoy the book, employ the strategies and celebrate success with your pupils.

Gordon Topping

Gordon Topping
Chief Executive
North Eastern Education and Library Board

INVESTOR IN PEOPLE

This book has evolved from a series of presentations given in schools and colleges in the North-Eastern Education and Library Board on Effective Learning and Teaching.

It is based on recent research into how children learn and the role of the different parts of the brain and senses in learning. It rapidly became apparent that children need to be equal partners in the learning process and require a full understanding of how this comes about.

We hope this book will serve to increase awareness of pupils about their own learning styles and empower them to take control of their learning.

We would like to acknowledge the contribution of all who participated in the production.
In particular **Tom McGlinchey**, Graphic Designer NEELB for the layout and graphics.
A special thanks to **Carmel Gallagher**, Deputy Director Curriculum, CCEA for her professional advice and support.

We are particularly indebted to the sponsor namely Northern Ireland Council for Curriculum Examinations and Assessment (CCEA) who has generously contributed to the costs of production.

Sean Maguire

Sean Maguire
General Adviser, Science and Technology, NEELB

Heather Thompson

Heather Thompson
General Adviser, School Improvement, NEELB.

'The greatest unexplored territory is the space between our ears'. Bill O Brien

'Understanding a child's brain and the way it develops is the key to understanding learning' Jane Healy 'Your child's mind'

A well-developed mind, a passion to learn and an ability to put knowledge to work are the keys to the future... Scans Report 'What work requires of schools'.

These quotations are taken from an array of books for teachers, parents and the general public, aimed at helping us understand how our brain works in order to help improve young people's capacity to learn. Few, if any, of these have been aimed directly at young people themselves.

When CCEA became aware of NEELB's plans to provide a publication specifically for young people in the North Eastern Board area, the Council was anxious to support the initiative in a way that would allow schools across Northern Ireland to benefit from the work. The authors of this book are aware that neuroscience is in its infancy and that new discoveries are being made all the time. On occasions these can contradict what has been discovered the previous month. On the other hand it seems foolish to wait until we are absolutely certain about everything, before we start to convey to young people some of the basics about how the brain works and how this impacts on their learning.

CCEA is therefore delighted to support this initiative, which tries, in a straightforward and colourful way, to give young people some basic insights into how the brain works and their capacity to learn better. We hope that this publication will be the first of a series on how to improve young people's self esteem, motivation, learning skills and overall potential.

Gavin Boyd
Chief Executive, CEA.

Sean Maguire
General Adviser, Science and Technology, NEELB

Heather Thompson
General Adviser, School Improvement, NEELB.

Developing People for Life

Rewarding Learning

2

CONTENTS

"Today, the greatest single source of wealth is between your ears. Today wealth is contained in brainpower not brutepower"

Brian Tracy author of Maximum Achievement

OUR BRILLIANT BRAINS

Did you know that no computer yet built is as powerful as the human brain?

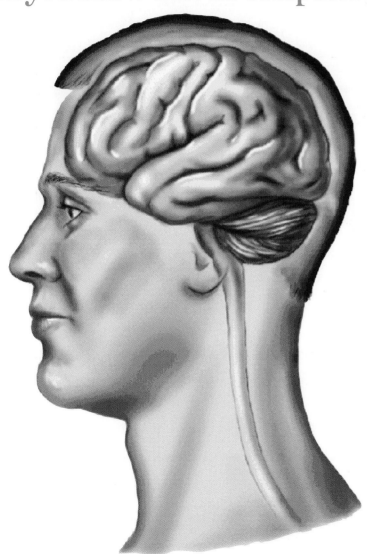

The potential for developing our brains is unlimited - we just need to keep using them!

Over 80% of what we understand about how the human brain works has been discovered in the past 10 years. This is because of MRI (Magnetic Resonance Imaging) scans and CAT (Computerised Axial Tomography) scans which can detect the parts of the brain that are active during thinking and learning.

This new knowledge about how the brain works will help you to learn much more effectively.

THE LEARNING BRAIN

Do you know about the learning parts of your brain?

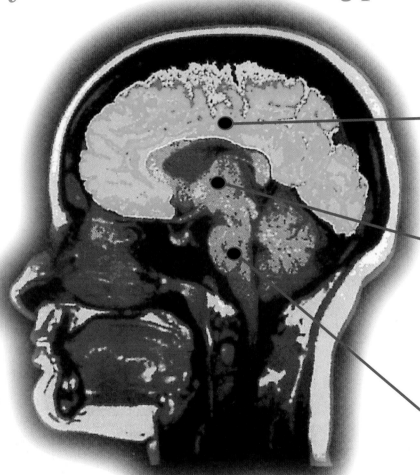

Different parts of the brain interact to allow us to learn.

The Neo-Cortex - this is where higher order thinking skills such as problem-solving take place. Here the brain works out patterns and meaning.

The Limbic System - this is the seat of the emotions and long term memory. We remember best when we use our emotions in learning.

There is a part of the brain which can slow down or prevent learning from taking place:

The Reptilian Brain (brainstem) - this part of the brain looks after our basic survival. Under stress the Reptilian Brain blocks the Neo-Cortex and the Limbic System from thinking and remembering, so that learning is slowed down or prevented.

THE REPTILIAN BRAIN
Did you know that stress causes us to "go reptilian"?

The reptilian brain is so called because it is the most primitive part of our brain. Under stress the reptilian brain takes over and we react in one of the following ways:

Fight - We become aggressive. Have you ever seen anyone lose their temper with another pupil or teacher?

Flight - We run away from a stressful situation. Have you ever seen a pupil bolt for the door without thinking?

Freeze - We are unable to move or speak. Have you ever watched a pupil panic, become speechless and unable to think?

"If you are in any of the above states no learning is taking place!"

EFFECTIVE LEARNING
Are you a super cool learner?

You learn best when you:

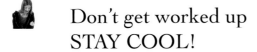 Don't get worked up
STAY COOL!

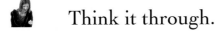 Think it through.

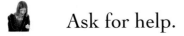 Ask for help.

Feel good about yourself.

Do relaxation exercises.

Learn how to handle stress.

Plan your work. Avoid
letting homeworks pile up!

 Enjoy your
learning.

 Set and
meet learning targets.

 Make time for your friends.

 Stay fit and healthy.

 Drink lots of fresh water.

 Reward yourself during study breaks with a snack.

 Use music to improve your learning.

"Now you are learning!"

EFFECTIVE LEARNING

Do you become involved in your learning?
Do you join in and enjoy your learning?
The more your emotions are involved the more likely you are to remember.

Learning will be long term if it:

- seems relevant to you.

- excites you and stimulates your imagination.

- stimulates your emotions.

- is connected with something you care about.

- brings back memories of a place, a sound, a feeling, a smell or an event.

- makes you want to find out more.

- challenges you to think.

"Memories are made of this!"

CONNECTING LEARNING
What happens when we are thinking and learning?

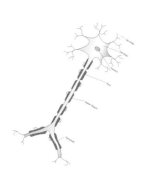

Our brains contain billions of nerve cells or neurons which send electrical and chemical messages to one another.

Connected neurons form permanent learning pathways in our brains - long term memory.

Examples of permanent learning pathways include:

- knowing the alphabet.
- knowing your tables for maths.
- writing.
- using a keyboard.
- tying your shoelace.
- riding your bike.
- driving a car.

"Now remember this!"

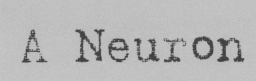

Dendrites

Cell Body

Nucleus

Axon

Myelin Sheath

Synapses

A Neuron

CONNECTING THE NEURONS

Do you know how to improve your long term memory?

Learning pathways are created when we use the information to be learned or the skill to be mastered in different ways for example,

say the information out loud.

explain it to a friend.

structure the information under meaningful headings.

put the information up around your room or house on pages or "post-its" and move around when learning.

draw the information on to a mind map or diagram.

make up a tune, a rap, a poem, a rhyme.

Nerve cells in the brain linked together.

"I'm gonna get myself connected"

RIGHT AND LEFT BRAIN

Does your right brain know what your left brain is doing?

The neo cortex is divided into two hemispheres - the Right Brain and the Left Brain. Some of us use one side of our brains more than the other.

Left Brain

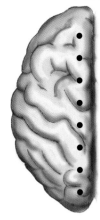

- Words - Language
- Numbers
- Logic
- Sequence
- Writing
- Reading
- Maths
- Fine detail

Right Brain

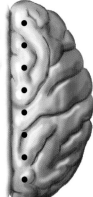

- Creativity
- Visualisation
- Patterns
- Images and Pictures
- Perspective / Dimension
- Music
- Rhyme and Rhythm
- Art and Design
- Big Picture

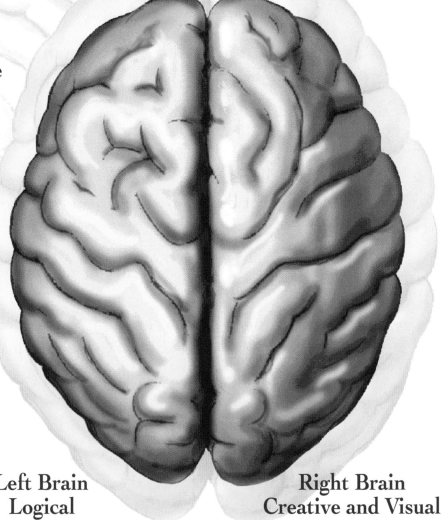

**Left Brain
Logical**

**Right Brain
Creative and Visual**

"Bridge that Gap"

WHOLE BRAIN LEARNING

Do you understand how physical exercise will stimulate your brain?

Our best learning takes place when we use both our right and left brains - whole brain learning.

Brain Gym

One way to improve the connections between the two sides of the brain is to do exercises called brain gym. These exercises work because the right brain controls the left side of the body and vice versa.

For Example:

- Pat your head with your right hand and rub your stomach with your left hand - do this 20 times, then swap round your hands and this time rub your head and pat your stomach - 20 times.

- Brain gym also increases the blood flow to the brain. This means that there is more oxygen available to the neurons. Our brains need oxygen to learn. Any physical exercise will improve blood flow to the brain.

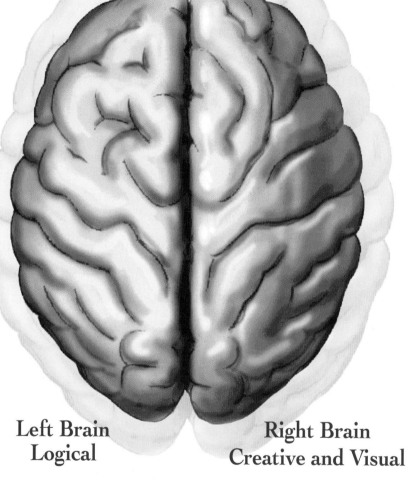

Left Brain
Logical

Right Brain
Creative and Visual

"Pump those neurons"

FOOD AND DRINK

Do you ever feel sleepy in school and find it difficult to learn?
Could your brain be hungry or thirsty?

 Our brains, like the rest of our bodies,
become dehydrated if we do not drink enough water.
Dehydrated brains cannot learn!

 Drink plenty of water throughout the day.

 Eat a healthy diet! Foods like fish, nuts,
fruit, vegetables and lean meat nourish the brain
and help it to learn.

"Food for thought"

LEARNING STYLES

Do you know that we learn in different ways?

Our brains process information in three ways:

 Visual - Some of us learn better through seeing pictures diagrams, moving images and colour.

 Auditory - Some of us learn better through hearing sounds and voices.

 Kinesthetic - Some of us learn better through doing, moving and touching.

We all use these three learning styles. Some of us prefer to learn in one or two of these ways. These are our learning preference(s) or preferred learning style(s). It is important to think about your preferred learning styles and develop the methods of learning which suit you best.

 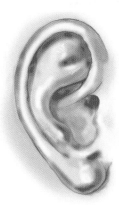 

"I learned it my way"

15

LEARNING STYLES
Are you a visual learner?
Do you like colour, images and shape?

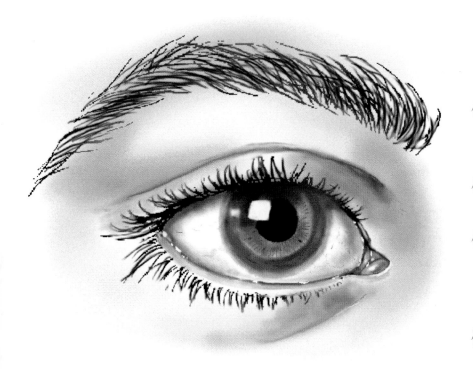

Visual learners

29% of us prefer to learn by storing images in our brains.

Visual Learners should:

use pictures, mind maps, computers, diagrams, flowcharts, key words, TV, videos, mind maps.

use colour to help the brain remember.

use different coloured pens and pencils to colour diagrams and when writing notes use highlighter pens to highlight text.

write information in bullet points or as key words on "post-its" - (they come in different colours).

"See how you learn!"

LEARNING STYLES

Are you an auditory learner? Do you respond to sounds and noises?

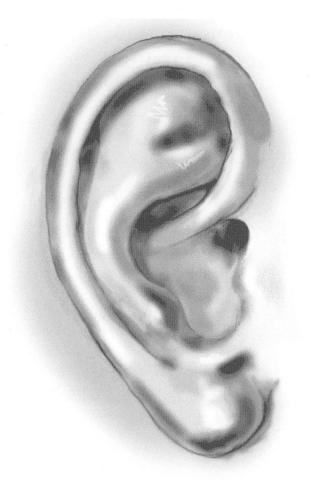

Auditory learners

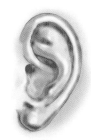

34% of us prefer to learn by storing sounds in our brains.

Auditory learners should:

- learn with friends - talk over the work and help each other to understand it.

- tape notes and play them back.

- listen to music while learning.

- repeat their work out loud.

- repeat their work out loud in funny voices.

- make up rhymes or raps about their work.

- get someone in their family to ask them questions about the work

- use DVDs, CD-Roms and computer programs from which they can hear the text spoken as they read.

"Have you got your ears on?"

LEARNING STYLES

Do you like to move when learning?
Do you like to touch objects or use computers when learning?

37% of us prefer to learn by movement or touch.

Kinesthetic learners should:

Kinesthetic learners

- where possible touch, feel or do things practically.

- use computers.

- put their notes on cards or "post-its" and sequence them. (perhaps rank the cards in order of importance or make into sentences).

- walk between notes or "post-its" that are on the floor or on the walls.

- walk around while reading.

- do brain gym exercises.

- stand up - stretch or exercise - at least every 20 minutes.

- draw pictures, mind maps - run a finger between the words on the map, say each one out loud.

- squeeze a sponge or stress release ball while working.

"Make learning a moving experience"

MULTIPLE INTELLIGENCES

It's not how smart you are that matters, what really counts is
"how are you smart?"

According to Howard Gardner we have eight different intelligences, for example some of us have a highly developed mathematical intelligence, some have a highly developed kinesthetic intelligence, others a highly developed musical intelligence. We are capable of developing a range of these intelligences given opportunity and encouragement.

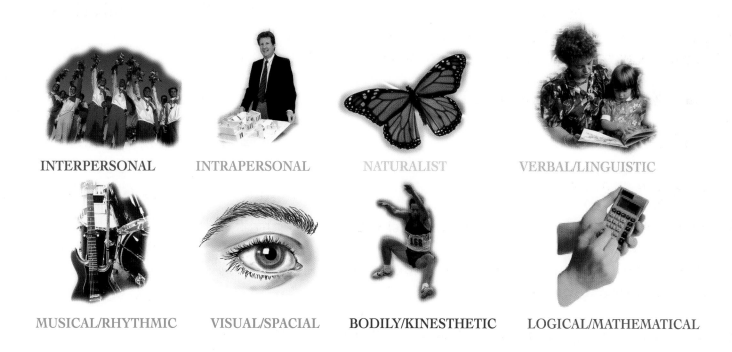

INTERPERSONAL	INTRAPERSONAL	NATURALIST	VERBAL/LINGUISTIC
MUSICAL/RHYTHMIC	VISUAL/SPACIAL	BODILY/KINESTHETIC	LOGICAL/MATHEMATICAL

"How Are You Smart?"

MULTIPLE INTELLIGENCES
How Are You Smart?

Logical / Mathematical
People with a strong mathematical / logical intelligence are good with numbers and recognise patterns quickly, **(developed through**, for example, problem solving, sequencing - putting things in order, puzzles, awareness of numbers all around us).

Verbal / Linguistic
People with a strong verbal/ linguistic intelligence are good with words and language - they read and write easily, (developed through, for example, story telling - both oral and written, writing activities, building up vocabulary, discussion and debate).

Bodily / Kinesthetic
People with a strong bodily / kinesthetic intelligence enjoy physical movement and are good at sport, dance and drama. **(developed through,** for example, working with objects, role play / drama, brain gym, field trips, sport).

Visual / Spatial Intelligence
People with a strong visual / spatial intelligence are good at thinking in pictures (visualising), design, charts, diagrams, pictures and maps, (developed through, for example, drawing, design, mind mapping, ICT, using colour, diagrams, pictures, visualisation, display vocabulary, mathematical / scientific formula).

"Work smarter - naturally"

MULTIPLE INTELLIGENCES
How Are You Smart?

Naturalist

People with a strong naturalist intelligence are interested in anything to do with the natural world, (developed through, for example, relating work to nature, classification).

Musical / Rhythmical

People with a strong musical intelligence are sensitive to pitch, tone and rhythm, play an instrument, enjoy listening to music, (developed through, for example, composing songs, raps. Use music in background for learning and for motivation using rhythm).

Intrapersonal

People who can work and solve problems on their own - like to plan and get on with their own work, (developed through, for example, making the work have personal meaning e.g. relate every topic to home or interests, personal goal setting and target setting, self-assessment).

Interpersonal

People who work well with others in groups or teams - like group work in school, solving problems with others. (developed through, for example, group work, role play, group discussions, team games).

"Work smarter - naturally"

EMOTIONAL INTELLIGENCE
Why is Emotional Intelligence important to you?

Emotionally intelligent people have well developed interpersonal and intrapersonal intelligences.

They:
- are team players.
- listen well.
- lead others.
- are friendly and outgoing.
- like to work and learn in groups.
- understand and manage their emotions.
- value relationships.
- value feedback from others.
- set and work towards targets.
- are self-confident and self-motvated.

There is increasing evidence to suggest that emotional intelligence is a much better indicator of success in life and in work than academic intelligence.

Young people who learn to handle their emotions will do better in school and do better in life after school.

You should be aware of and attempt to develop your emotional intelligence.

"Use your emotional intelligence"

THE ACCELERATED LEARNING CYCLE

Do you ask yourself questions about why you are learning?
Do you ask yourself the questions in the learning cycle?

connect the learning  BIG Picture First

What have you already learned about this topic?

Where does this topic fit in with your work for the year or the exam specification? Will it help you achieve targets?

review for reflection and retention

Do you ask yourself questions to test if you have achieved your learning outcomes?

Learning Cycle

What do you want to know by the end of this piece of work?

describe the outcomes

activity   input

demonstrate

Could you teach this topic to other pupils?

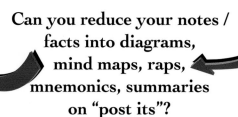

Can you reduce your notes / facts into diagrams, mind maps, raps, mnemonics, summaries on "post its"?

after Alistair Smith

"Learning is not a one stop shop"

MUSIC AND LEARNING
Do you ever listen to music when learning?
Did you know that the right sort of music improves learning?

Relaxed brains learn more effectively. Music can help your brain prepare for learning.

Research shows that playing music by Mozart stimulates the brain.

Other pieces that are good to listen to while studying are:

- Vivaldi: 'The Four Seasons'
- Enya: L'Esprit - 'Far Island'
- Bach: 'Concerto for Harp in F Major'

When you want to motivate yourself before a test or exam play music like:

- Vangelis: 'Chariots of Fire'
- Heather Small: 'What did you do today to make you feel proud?'
- M-People: 'Search for the hero inside yourself'

BACH

"Soothe those neurons"

SELF ESTEEM
How do you feel about yourself?

High self esteem means you:

- 😊 feel confident about yourself and your school work.

- 😊 have the confidence to make mistakes and to learn from them.

- 😊 are positive in your outlook on life - an optimist.

- 😊 believe you are a winner.

Low self esteem means you:

- ☹️ feel less confident about yourself and your school work.

- ☹️ dread making mistakes which you see as failure.

- ☹️ are negative in your outlook on life - a pessimist.

- ☹️ believe you are a loser.

"Reach out... and stretch yourself"

SELF ESTEEM How do you improve it?

Research shows that pupils with high self esteem are more successful learners. You can improve your self esteem by:

- ☑ planning for and expecting success.

- ☑ using positive language.

- ☑ thinking positive thoughts about yourself and others.

- ☑ ignoring put downs.

- ☑ seeing yourself as a success at school and in your life.

- ☑ setting yourself goals.

- ☑ helping and encouraging each other with your learning.

- ☑ learning from your mistakes - everyone makes mistakes - the key is to use them to learn.

- ☑ look for the hero inside yourself - THINK!! What have you done today to make you feel proud?

"Keep your face to the sunshine and you cannot see the shadow"

(Helen Keller)

Positive Language

Do you use negative language?
Do you know how to change it to positive language?

Negative

Positive

Negative	Positive
'I can't do that'	'I will be able to do that'
'But I got 10 out of 20 wrong'	'and I got 10 out of 20 correct'
'I don't understand any of that'	'Please explain this part which I don't understand'

"I will because I can"

27

POSITIVE AFFIRMATION
Do you think positively?

Choose positive affirmations (statements) which you can look at, put them on your bedroom wall, stick on to your notebooks / pencil case or write them round your timetable. Ask someone to write something good about you.

AFFIRMATIONS

A problem? - Create your solution.

'Simply the best!'

Think big-then just do it

Success comes in cans not in can't.

'Reach for the sky'

'I am so clever that the computer has not been made that can do what I can do!'

'Go for it!'

A smile is my style.

'The thing always happens that you really believe in and the belief in the thing makes it happen.'
Frank Lloyd Wright (famous architect)

"You can do it if you only knew it"

TARGET SETTING
What are Goals, Targets, Tasks?
What's in it for me?

Goals..... where you want to be in the long term - the destination.

Targets.. steps on the way to goals.

Tasks..... work to be done to meet targets.

Think about:

- the future - identify goals.

- the results you want - identify targets.

- the tasks needed to make your goals and targets happen - write them down and review your progress regularly.

- visualing success. What does it look like?

- how success feels.

- hearing people congratulate you on your success. What are they saying?

"Aim high - go for it!"

IMPROVE YOUR MEMORY
Do you forget things quickly?

Most of us are all good at short term memory (remembering things for a brief period), but not so good at long term memory!

Use some of these memory techniques to help you to store information in your long term memory:

make a story -
> turn your learning into a story.

mind maps -
> mind maps (using keywords) help you to classify.

rhymes -
> make up rhymes to help you to remember - put the words to music.

classification -
> placing similar words together under headings.

mnemonics -
> associating ideas, numbers with words;
> ie.   North East South West
>   Now Every Student Wins

Every time I learn something new it pushes some old stuff out of my brain!

repetition-
- repeat your work in different ways.
- write or draw it in different colours.
- say it out loud.
- walk around and repeat it.

"Remember in time with a well designed rhyme"

MIND MAPS AND MEMORY
How do mind maps help you access the information in your brain?

Mind Maps are a way of using keywords.

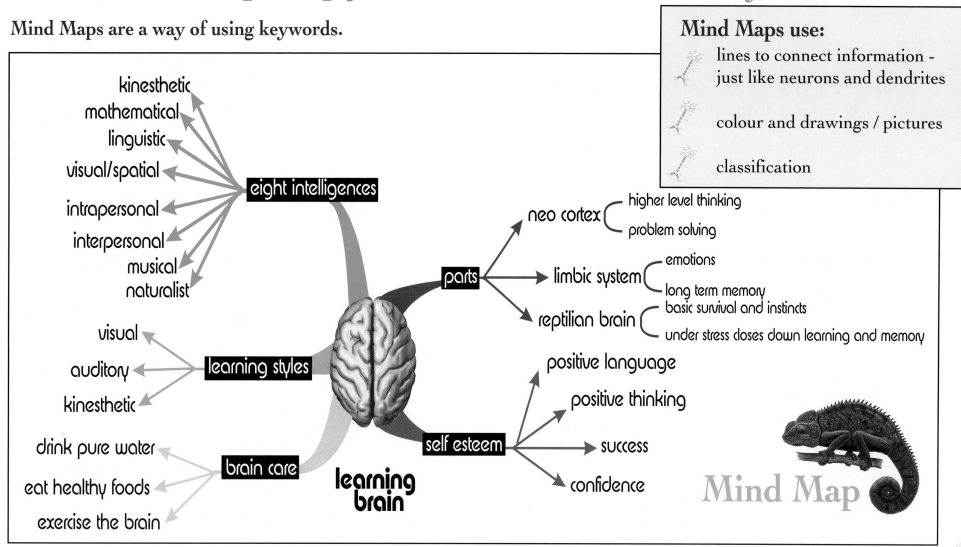

Mind Maps use:
- lines to connect information - just like neurons and dendrites
- colour and drawings / pictures
- classification

kinesthetic
mathematical
linguistic
visual/spatial
intrapersonal
interpersonal
musical
naturalist

eight intelligences

visual
auditory
kinesthetic

learning styles

drink pure water
eat healthy foods
exercise the brain

brain care

learning brain

parts

neo cortex — higher level thinking, problem solving

limbic system — emotions, long term memory

reptilian brain — basic survival and instincts, under stress closes down learning and memory

self esteem

positive language
positive thinking
success
confidence

Mind Map

"In the Mind's Eye"

Resources

These are books and websites which you, your teachers and parents could read to find out more about learning:

BOOKS

Accelerate your Learning, Six Super Skills, Rose and Gole, Accelerated Learning Systems, ISBN 0-905553-41-1

Accelerate your Learning, Rose and Gole, Accelerated Learning Systems, ISBN 0-905553-40-3

Accelerated Learning for the 21st Century, Rose and Nicholl, Judy Piatkus Publishers Ltd., ISBN 0-7499-1762-8

The Learning Revolution, Dryden and Voss, The Learning Web, ISBN 0-9583701-0-9

Emotional Intelligence, Daniel Goldman, Bloomsbury Publishing plc., ISBN 0-7475-2830-6

Accelerated Learning in Practice, Alistair Smith, Network Educational Press, ISBN 1-855-39-048-5

Accelerated Learning in The Classroom, Alistair Smith, Network Educational Press, ISBN 1-855-39-034-5

ALPS - Accelerated Learning in Schools, Alistair Smith and Nicola Call, ISBN1-855-39-056-6 , Network Educational Press

The Alps Approach, Alistair Smith and Nicola Call, Network Educational Press, ISBN 1-85539-078-7

Effective Teaching and Learning in the Primary Classroom, Shaw and Hawks, Optimal Learning, ISBN 095-335-31-0-9

Mapwise, Caviglioli & Harris, Network Educational Press, ISBN 1855-39-0590

The Learning File, University of Strathclyde

The M.I. Strategy Bank, Ellen Arnold, Zephyr, ISBN 1-56976-097-7

Brain-Based Learning, Turning Point Pub., ISBN 0-9637832-1-1